CW01431698

Original title:
Journey Through the Radiant

Author: Eliora Lumiste
ISBN HARDBACK: 978-1-80561-236-0
ISBN PAPERBACK: 978-1-80561-797-6

Echoes of Radiance in Every Step

In each step I take, a whisper flows,
Carried by winds where the wild grass grows.
Sunlight dances on paths I've wandered,
In moments of joy, my spirit pondered.

Through valleys deep, where shadows play,
I find the light, chasing clouds away.
Every heartbeat sings a song,
Of love and hope, where we belong.

The Colors of the Awakened Heart

Awakened hues paint the morning sky,
Brushstrokes of longing, as time drifts by.
With every breath, the world ignites,
In softest colors, my spirit delights.

Scarlet and gold in the dawn's embrace,
Every moment a vibrant trace.
The whispers of love, a tender hue,
In the palette of life, I'm born anew.

Fragments of Light in the Silent Spaces

In silent corners, where shadows dwell,
Fragments of light weave stories to tell.
Glimmers of hope in the stillness found,
Whispers of truth in the gentle sound.

The quiet speaks in a language rare,
Echoes of dreams float through the air.
In these moments, my heart takes flight,
Finding the beauty in soft twilight.

The Radiant Whirl of Existence

Life spins in circles, a dance so bright,
Radiant patterns beneath the night.
Every turn, a chance to feel,
The pulse of existence, so vivid, so real.

With every laugh, a spark ignites,
In this whirl of joy, our spirit invites.
Together we twirl in the cosmic flow,
The dance of the universe, forever aglow.

Shattering Darkness with Luminous Journeys

In the depths where shadows play,
A flicker stirs, a break of day.
Step by step, the light will lead,
Chasing doubts, receding need.

With every breath, a spark ignites,
Illuming paths, dispelling nights.
Through valleys low and mountains high,
We rise beyond the darkened sky.

The Weightlessness of Shining Moments

In laughter shared and whispers sweet,
Time dances lightly, hearts entreat.
Moments fleeting, yet profound,
In silence, joy is often found.

Each thread a memory we weave,
In weightless grace, we dare believe.
With every glance, our spirits soar,
The shining moments we adore.

Veins of Light in the Earth's Heart

Deep beneath the surface lies,
A pulse of glow, where silence cries.
Veins of light in shadows dwell,
Whispering secrets, tales to tell.

From roots that seek, to branches wide,
In earthy depths, our dreams reside.
The heartbeat of the world alive,
In every vein, our hopes survive.

Where the Stars Whisper Secrets

In the night where silence reigns,
Stars unveil their quiet gains.
Softly tucked in cosmic lace,
Whispers travel through the space.

Each twinkle holds a tale untold,
Ancient truths in starlight bold.
In celestial arms, we find repose,
Secrets shared where darkness flows.

The Odyssey of Shimmering Skies

Beneath the vast, enchanting dome,
Waves of azure gently roam.
A journey begins in twilight's grace,
Chasing dreams in this endless space.

Clouds of silver softly drift,
In shadows where the heart can lift.
Each star a beacon, shining bright,
Guiding souls through the velvet night.

Whispers of winds play a sweet tune,
Carrying tales to the glowing moon.
A path unfolds, mysterious and wide,
In shimmering skies where dreams reside.

Time flows like rivers, swift and clear,
Each moment holds both joy and fear.
Onward we sail, with spirits high,
In the odyssey of the shimmering sky.

As dawn breaks with golden rays,
We find solace in the sun's warm gaze.
For in this odyssey, we renew,
With shimmering skies, our hearts break through.

Echoes of a Gilded Trail

In the woods where secrets lie,
Footsteps whisper, soft as sighs.
Leaves adorned in hues of gold,
Echo stories yet untold.

Sunlight dances through the trees,
Carried gently on the breeze.
Nature hums a lovely tune,
As daylight melts into the moon.

Every turn a tale to weave,
Of cherished moments, we believe.
Each echo lingers in the air,
A gilded trail, forever rare.

In shadows, laughter finds its place,
A tapestry of time and space.
We follow paths, both old and new,
On echoes of a trail imbued.

With every step, an adventure calls,
As whispered echoes fill the halls.
We wander forth, with hearts unveiled,
On life's journey, a gilded trail.

Starlit Footsteps on Silent Waves

Upon the shore, where dreams arise,
We tread the sands under starlit skies.
Whispers of ocean in the night,
Call our hearts to dance with light.

Each step a note in the cosmic swell,
Stories of lovers the moon will tell.
Silent waves embrace the shore,
With every tide, we crave for more.

Reflections shimmer on the sea,
Illuminating what's meant to be.
In this moment, time stands still,
As starlit footprints trace the thrill.

With every wave, the world unfolds,
A symphony in twilight's hold.
Guided by stars, we find our way,
Through starlit footsteps, night turns day.

In tranquil dreams, we drift and sway,
Carried forth by the ocean's play.
Together we roam, hearts ablaze,
On silent waves, in starlit haze.

Discovering the Luster of Tomorrow

In the hush of dawn's embrace,
We seek the dreams that time will trace.
With open hearts and eager minds,
The luster of tomorrow, we hope to find.

Each sunrise paints the world anew,
With colors bright and glimmers true.
A canvas waiting for our touch,
In moments small, we discover much.

Futures whisper on the breeze,
In every rustle of the trees.
Guided steps and visions clear,
Unravel paths year after year.

In the dance of life, we take a chance,
With every twirl, we learn to dance.
The luster shines in laughter shared,
In bonds of love that show we cared.

Tomorrow's promise glimmers bright,
Inviting us to chase the light.
Together we stride, hand in hand,
Discovering luster in this land.

Rolling Hills of Polished Light

In the dawn's embrace, shadows play,
Glowing hills greet the breaking day.
Whispers of wind through emerald blades,
Chasing the night as daylight fades.

Golden hues dance on the land,
Nature's canvas, gentle and grand.
Waves of grass, a soft delight,
Rolling hills of polished light.

Pines stand tall, guardians wise,
Beneath their watch, the world will rise.
Every peak, a story told,
In whispers soft, in colors bold.

Distant mountains cradle the sky,
Dreams take flight, oh, how they fly!
Through valleys deep, the rivers wend,
In harmony, all paths blend.

As twilight falls, stars ignite,
Illuminating the tranquil night.
In this realm, hearts feel so light,
Rolling hills, forever bright.

Fragments of a Visionary Expedition

Amidst the ruins, shadows loom,
Whispers echo in the crowded room.
Pieces scattered, a puzzle rare,
Glimmers of dreams linger in the air.

Across the landscape, echoes call,
Each step forward, a chance to fall.
With every heartbeat, courage grows,
Unlocking paths that no one knows.

Visions dance, like fireflies bright,
Guiding seekers through the night.
Fragments join in the mind's design,
Crafting worlds, both yours and mine.

Through forests lush and mountains steep,
Awakening secrets that time will keep.
Every journey, a tale to weave,
In the heart's fabric, we believe.

Eager spirits, rising high,
Chasing horizons, we will fly.
Through every struggle, every quest,
In fragments found, we are our best.

Chronicles of the Brilliance Found

In whispers soft and shadows deep,
A story waits, a secret to keep.
From ashes rise, the tales unfold,
Of dreams once lost, now brave and bold.

Through tangled woods and hidden streams,
The heart awakens, reigniting dreams.
Each footstep soft, a gentle sigh,
Guiding the soul toward the sky.

With every star that paints the night,
A flicker born, a spark of light.
In fearless hearts the courage grows,
To chase the path that fate bestows.

In twilight hues, the dawn is near,
A melody that whispers clear.
The brilliance found, a flame anew,
Guided by hope, forever true.

As echoes fade, the journey swells,
In stories told, what magic dwells.
Through chronicles of the brave and wise,
The spirit soars, beneath the skies.

Navigating Through the Golden Veil

A world aglow with liquid gold,
Where dreams are spun and tales unfold.
Through gentle mists and radiant light,
We seek the dawn beyond the night.

With every step, the shadows tease,
Yet inner strength brings hearts at ease.
Waves of warmth, a soft embrace,
In every heartbeat, we find our place.

Beneath the veil, the whispers play,
Guiding our souls, they light the way.
In this realm of shifting sands,
Together bound, we take our stands.

The stories woven in threads of fate,
Lead us to realms that wait and create.
In every glance, there lies a chance,
To join the dance of a timeless romance.

Through golden hues, our spirits soar,
Embracing love forevermore.
In every heartbeat, we unveil,
The beauty found in the golden veil.

Spheres of Light in Quiet Corners

In hidden nooks where shadows play,
Spheres of light dance in disarray.
A whisper calls through stillness profound,
In every heart, a magic found.

Soft luminescence breaks the dark,
Illuminating dreams that spark.
With gentle grace, the night aligns,
In quiet corners, the heart defines.

Through tangled thoughts, the pathways weave,
A tapestry of what we believe.
Each sphere of light, a guiding flame,
In moments shared, we know our name.

In twilight's hush, reflections mirror,
The quiet truth that shines much clearer.
As shadows fade, the voices rise,
In spheres of light, we claim the skies.

Connected souls in twilight's glow,
Through quiet corners, love will flow.
With every breath, the light ignites,
In unity, we dance through nights.

Embracing the Ethereal Path

In whispers of the winds that call,
We find our journey, we heed the thrall.
With open hearts, we take each stride,
Embracing the path where dreams abide.

Through valleys deep and mountains high,
Underneath the ever-changing sky.
We thread the needle of fate's own seam,
With every heartbeat, we chase the dream.

The stars above, a guiding light,
Illuminating the endless night.
In every step, a truth revealed,
As courage born, our fate is sealed.

Through storms we dance, through fires we tread,
All fears succumb to the dreams we've fed.
In every moment, we choose to feel,
The ethereal path, our spirits heal.

With love as our compass, we roam afar,
Chasing the magic beneath each star.
Together we move, through shadows we glide,
Embracing the path where hopes reside.

The Flickering Compass Within

A whisper in the dark, it calls,
Guiding hearts through shadowed halls.
An ember's glow, a flicker's guide,
In silence deep, where dreams abide.

Through storms that rage and shadows play,
It points the course, come what may.
In quest of truth, in search of light,
The compass stirs, igniting night.

With every turn and subtle sign,
It leads the lost, connects the vine.
In stillness found, the moment clear,
The flicker shines, dissolving fear.

Each heartbeat beats a rhythmic thrum,
Awakening paths yet to come.
Inward journeys, brave and free,
Reveal the spark of who we be.

So trust the compass, let it show,
The way through life, the ebb and flow.
For every heart has its own light,
A flickering compass, shining bright.

Glows and Grooves in the Cosmic Dance

In cosmic realms where stars collide,
Galaxies twirl on velvet tide.
Each twinkle hums a timeless tune,
Dancing brightly beneath the moon.

A rhythm sways in brilliant hues,
Painting skies with vibrant views.
The universe, a grand ballet,
In glowing arcs, it finds its way.

Planets spin in graceful trance,
Embracing fate in cosmic chance.
With every pulse, the stardust swirls,
Creating magic in swirling whirl.

Through every beat, the heavens glow,
Revealing secrets we long to know.
With every groove, we sway and spin,
Lost in the beauty woven within.

Together we dance, both near and far,
Guided by the light of each shining star.
In the night's embrace, we find our stance,
Glows and grooves in the cosmic dance.

Landscapes of Illumination

Across the hills, the sunbeams break,
Awakening fields, the world we make.
Each blade of grass, a story told,
In vibrant colors, lush and bold.

Mountains rise like ancient shields,
Guarding secrets that nature yields.
With every sunset, shadows play,
Crafting wonders at end of day.

Rivers wind with silver flows,
Mirroring skies in tranquil prose.
The whispers of the woods ignite,
In landscapes painted soft with light.

From meadows bright to valleys deep,
Where dreams emerge in twilight's keep.
Each corner turned reveals a spark,
In landscapes vast, where shadows Lark.

So wander forth, let beauty bloom,
Embrace the light, dispel the gloom.
For in each step, the world unfurls,
A tapestry of vibrant swirls.

Treading the Firefly Lane

In dusk's embrace, the fireflies glow,
Guiding us through the soft, dark flow.
With twinkling lights in gentle air,
They dance around without a care.

Each flicker calls, a secret shared,
Whispers of dreams that are dared.
Through leafy trails and twilight's play,
We tread softly on firefly lane.

Their magic glows in patterns bright,
Leading the way through gentle night.
Each moment a spark, ephemeral grace,
In luminous trails, we find our place.

Hand in hand, we journey far,
Beneath the watchful evening star.
With every step, enchantment reigns,
As we wander through firefly lanes.

So let your heart flutter and soar,
Embrace the light forevermore.
For in this dance, we intertwine,
In firefly's glow, your heart is mine.

A Tapestry of Celestial Colors

In skies of blue, the sun does rise,
With hues that dance where beauty lies.
Crimson clouds in golden light,
A tapestry woven, pure delight.

The moon whispers tales of silver sheen,
Among the stars, a tranquil scene.
Each starlet glimmers, a tiny spark,
Adorning the heavens, chasing the dark.

A river runs of colors bold,
Celestial stories waiting to unfold.
Through cosmic threads, the dreams all play,
In this vibrant world, night meets day.

Oceans of violet, emerald streams,
Nature's brush strokes, painting our dreams.
A gallery vast, where hearts entwine,
In the celestial chorus, we're all divine.

So let us gaze, let wonder ignite,
In this tapestry of purest light.
From dawn till dusk, let colors blend,
In harmony, we find our transcend.

Quest for the Guiding Star

Beneath the vast expanse we roam,
Searching for a light to call our home.
In the endless night, our path unclear,
We trust the star that draws us near.

Winds whisper secrets of the skies,
An ancient call that never lies.
The constellations map our fate,
With each twinkle, we eagerly await.

Through valleys deep and mountains high,
We soar on dreams, like birds we fly.
The guiding star, a beacon bright,
Illuminates the darkest night.

With every step, hope's flame we share,
A journey forged on love and care.
A bond unbroken through time and space,
Together we find our destined place.

In the cosmic dance, we'll take our stand,
With hearts united, we'll venture hand in hand.
For in this quest, we'll truly see,
The guiding star was always free.

Stray Sparks in the Velvet Night

In velvet night, the world is still,
As stray sparks dance upon the hill.
Whispers of dreams lost in the breeze,
Flickering softly through the trees.

With every shimmer, a story unfolds,
Of hopes and secrets the darkness holds.
In the quiet, magic starts to play,
A symphony of light, leading the way.

Like fireflies caught in a gentle flight,
They twirl and glide in their nightly rite.
Each spark a wish, a moment bright,
Illuminating shadows, banishing fright.

Boundless wonders in the night so deep,
Unseen treasures that softly seep.
In the stillness, we find our tune,
Awakening dreams beneath the moon.

As dawn approaches, they fade away,
Yet in our hearts, their glimmers stay.
With gratitude, we embrace the night,
For stray sparks remind us of inner light.

When Twilight Becomes a Canvas

When twilight arrives, the canvas glows,
With strokes of pink where the soft breeze blows.
Brushes of orange melt into blue,
A masterpiece crafted just for you.

The evening whispers, secrets unfold,
Telling stories that never get old.
In every shadow, a tale to find,
When twilight calls, we're free of mind.

Stars begin to peek at the darkened sky,
As the last rays of sunlight bid goodbye.
Each glimmer a promise, a wish made clear,
In twilight's embrace, we banish fear.

Colors merge in a waltz so sweet,
Hands held together, our hearts skip a beat.
In the fading light, we find our muse,
When twilight comes, we cannot lose.

So paint your dreams on this transient sheet,
As day meets night, life feels complete.
With every stroke, let your spirit soar,
When twilight whispers, forevermore.

A Song for the Celestial Wanderers

In the night, they take their flight,
Guided by the silver light.
Across the vastness they will roam,
Seeking the stars to call them home.

Waves of silence, whispers low,
Carry tales of worlds aglow.
Each heart beats with cosmic fire,
Yearning for a dream to inspire.

Through the void, they weave their path,
Dancing in the universe's math.
With every pulse, a new song starts,
Connecting endless wandering hearts.

In the tapestry of night they weave,
Stories of wonders we believe.
The cosmic symphony plays on,
Every note, a bond reborn.

Let us join these souls of grace,
In the endless celestial space.
Together, we'll chart the skies,
As wanderers with open eyes.

Between Starlight and Shadows

In the hush where shadows play,
Light whispers secrets of the day.
Between dusk and dawn, we stand,
Searching for a guiding hand.

Flickers soft, like dreams untold,
Bending time as we grow old.
Stars above, a million threads,
Stitched together where hope spreads.

Caught in the dance of dark and light,
We find a glimmer, hold it tight.
Every breath, a silent prayer,
Between the starlight, we share.

In the twilight's gentle hold,
Stories of the brave unfold.
Shadows whisper, secrets weave,
Hearts unite, as we believe.

A journey mapped in cosmic hues,
Between the paths that we must choose.
In starlit nights, we weave our fate,
Together, we illuminate.

Flares of Hope in Distant Realms

Across the galaxies, sparks ignite,
Flares of hope that chase the night.
In distant realms, where dreams are born,
Light breaks forth, a new dawn's sworn.

In every flicker, a promise glows,
To heal the scars that time bestows.
With courage stitched in every beam,
We chase the shadows, build a dream.

Through the dark, we journey far,
Guided by the light of a star.
With heart in hand, we dare to strive,
A tapestry of souls alive.

Among the echoes of the past,
Flares of hope forever last.
Each light a beacon, bright and true,
A call to arms for me and you.

So let us rise, united strong,
With flares of hope, we all belong.
In distant realms, our spirits soar,
Together, we will seek much more.

The Echoing Prism of Dreams

In the prism where colors collide,
Echoes of dreams we cannot hide.
Fragments of hopes, a vivid stream,
Merging magic with every gleam.

Let whispers carry us away,
To places where our wishes play.
Every hue holds a story bright,
Filling the canvas of the night.

In every shadow, a light remains,
Painting the silence, breaking chains.
Through prisms wide, we find our way,
Embracing the dreams that dare to stay.

With laughter woven in the air,
We touch the stars without a care.
The echoing depths of our desires,
Fuel the flames of eternal fires.

So take my hand, let's drift and glide,
Through the prism, side by side.
In dreams we trust, in light we beam,
Life's a canvas, paint your dream.

Pathways of Luminous Dreams

In twilight's gentle glow we tread,
Where shadows dance and whispers spread.
Each heartbeat echoes, a silent prayer,
Guiding us through the midnight air.

Stars above, like lanterns bright,
Illuminating paths in the night.
We wander on with souls aglow,
In search of places we long to know.

The moon reflects our hopes untold,
As stories linger, warm and bold.
With every step, the world unfolds,
A tapestry of dreams and gold.

In moments still, we find the key,
To unlock doors of destiny.
And in the silence, truth will gleam,
A guiding light, our cherished dream.

So take my hand, together we'll roam,
Through pathways rich, we'll find our home.
With every breath, a new design,
In luminous dreams, our hearts align.

Whispers of the Glowing Horizon

As dawn ignites the waking sky,
Whispers soft, they drift and fly.
The horizon glows, a canvas bright,
Painting hope with strokes of light.

Gentle breezes carry song,
Inviting all the hearts along.
Each step we take feels like a dance,
In rhythm with the world's expanse.

With colors warm and shadows play,
We chase the night, embrace the day.
Together we'll explore this veil,
Where dreams unfold and spirits sail.

Glimmers of faith in every dawn,
Guiding us until the night is gone.
And through the mists, we'll find our way,
With whispers echoing, come what may.

So raise your gaze to skies above,
In every whisper, hear the love.
The glowing horizon calls us near,
To find the way, to conquer fear.

Navigating Celestial Currents

In oceans vast of starry night,
We sail on dreams, our hearts in flight.
Guided by the moon's soft beam,
Navigating through each silver stream.

With cosmic winds, we chart our course,
In search of truth, a vibrant source.
The constellations map our fate,
As time unfolds, we resonate.

Through nebulous veils, we gently glide,
With every wave, a trusted guide.
In stellar whispers, secrets shared,
Across the void, we're unprepared.

Yet courage blooms in starlit dreams,
As we embrace what destiny means.
In cosmic dance, we find our place,
With every challenge, a warm embrace.

So take the helm and sail with grace,
Through currents bright, in endless space.
Navigating the unknown with zeal,
In celestial realms, our spirits heal.

Light's Embrace on Forgotten Roads

On forgotten roads where shadows dwell,
Light's embrace casts a timeless spell.
We wander forth with spirits free,
Finding solace in each memory.

Beneath the boughs of ancient trees,
Whispers drift upon the breeze.
Every step unveils the truth,
Echoes of laughter, remnants of youth.

In moments past, we see the shine,
Of love and loss, both intertwined.
And with each turn, the heart expands,
As light unveils what time commands.

With gentle grace, the twilight glows,
Revealing tales the universe knows.
Through every crack in dusty stone,
Resides a light that feels like home.

So walk with me along this trail,
Feel the magic in each exhale.
For light will guide both near and far,
On forgotten roads where we are.

Mosaics of the Celestial Canvas

Stars twinkle like diamonds bright,
Colors blend in cosmic flight.
Nebulas bloom, a vibrant show,
Whispers of worlds we'll never know.

Galaxies swirl in spiraled grace,
In the dark, they find their place.
Each point of light a distant song,
Guiding dreams where we belong.

Comets trail their fleeting glow,
In their wake, a tale they'll sow.
In the vastness, secrets hum,
In the silence, the night's a drum.

Planets dance around their sun,
Timeless movement, never done.
Gravity's pull, a gentle sway,
In the darkness, night turns to day.

Canvas vast, a grand design,
Infinite stories intertwine.
Mosaics woven in the skies,
In the night, our wonder lies.

Where Light Meets the Unseen

In shadows deep, the whispers grow,
Where light retreats, secrets flow.
Fleeting glimmers, hidden grace,
In quiet corners, light finds its place.

Veil of night, a soft embrace,
Illuminates the unseen space.
Stars above in silent watch,
Guiding souls with their gentle touch.

Between the known and the obscure,
Lies a world both dark and pure.
With each flicker, truth unveils,
In the silence, the spirit sails.

Dancing rays and muted hues,
In the twilight, our heart renews.
Where light meets all that lies ahead,
We tread softly, where dreams are fed.

Journey forth, embrace the night,
Let your heart be your guiding light.
In every shadow, hope will gleam,
A dance between the seen and dream.

Dances of Dawn in Dusk's Embrace

As the sun dips, day retreats,
Night unfurls with gentle beats.
Colors blend in a soft array,
Embracing dusk, the end of day.

Whispers linger in twilight's air,
Promises form in dreams we share.
Stars emerge, the sky ignites,
A symphony of cosmic sights.

Shadows play beneath the trees,
Rustling leaves stir in the breeze.
Color fades into deeper blue,
As night wraps all in its hue.

Crickets chirp, a sweet refrain,
Nature sighs, forgetting pain.
The world pauses to catch its breath,
In this dance, life conquers death.

Dawn will rise, as it must do,
But for now, we revel in the view.
Dusk holds secrets, soft and vast,
A moment where the future meets the past.

A Journey Beneath the Stars

Step softly on this ancient ground,
Where echoes of the past abound.
Beneath the stars, our hearts will soar,
In the night, we seek for more.

Trails of light cross overhead,
Whispers guide where angels tread.
In the silence, we find our way,
Through worlds born of night and day.

Stories told by each bright spark,
Guiding travelers through the dark.
Hearts united beneath the skies,
In every glance, a thousand sighs.

Galactic paths, a cosmic dance,
Every moment holds a chance.
Beneath the vast, infinite dome,
We wander far, yet feel at home.

With each step, the universe calls,
In its embrace, our spirit sprawls.
Underneath the constellations' gleam,
We embark on life's sweetest dream.

Tides of Light on the Sea of Dreams

Whispers drift upon the foam,
Carried softly, a gentle home.
Moonlit paths, serene and bright,
Guide the soul through endless night.

Waves that shimmer, tales unfold,
Secrets hidden, longing bold.
Each crest dances, spirits soar,
A canvas painted, evermore.

In twilight's grasp, the stars awake,
Hearts entwined in dreams they make.
A lullaby of cosmic spheres,
Bringing solace, calming fears.

Gentle currents, ebb and flow,
In their grasp, we learn to grow.
With every tide, hope's embrace,
Reflects the light of love's grace.

Lost in silence, we find peace,
In the whispers, sweet release.
Together we ride this gentle sea,
Bound by dreams, eternally free.

Flickers of Hope in the Heartbeat of Time

In the shadows, a spark ignites,
Softly glowing through the nights.
Each heartbeat whispers, hold on tight,
For dawn will break, dispelling fright.

With every tick, the promise gleams,
Woven within our wildest dreams.
Moments woven, fate's design,
Flickers dancing, so divine.

Through the chaos, find your way,
Shimmering light to greet each day.
In the silence, hope may bloom,
Casting away the dusk of gloom.

Every tear and every sigh,
Gathered stars in a twilight sky.
Together, we share this breath of air,
Holding memories, rich and rare.

As time flows on, the heartbeats blend,
Flickers of hope that never end.
In the rhythm, we find our place,
Embraced in love's warm grace.

The Harmony of Radiating Souls

Notes of laughter fill the air,
Radiating warmth we share.
Hearts aligned in joyful song,
Together we weave where we belong.

In each glance, a story told,
Threads of silver, strands of gold.
Boundless echoes, spirits rise,
Creating magic, endless skies.

The rhythm flows, a gentle tide,
Uniting all, our hearts abide.
In the dance of life, we sway,
Together in unity, come what may.

With every laugh, with every tear,
Harmony draws us ever near.
In the silence, whispers sing,
Radiating love in everything.

A symphony of souls that blend,
Creating echoes that never end.
In the warmth of every embrace,
We find our peace, our resting place.

Embracing the Brush of Illumination

With each stroke, the canvas wakes,
A dance of colors, love it makes.
Light cascades on vivid dreams,
Illuminating life's quiet themes.

In shadows deep, a whisper calls,
The brush of light, it softly falls.
Every hue tells a tale anew,
In every heartbeat, moments imbue.

Brush the doubts with shades of bright,
Ignite the spark, unleash the light.
In swirling patterns, stories grow,
As light embraces, shadows flow.

With each layer, a world appears,
Strokes of joy, and drawn-out fears.
Holding space for dreams to bloom,
Inviting love to fill the room.

So gather 'round, let colors lead,
In the embrace of every need.
With a stroke of hope, we find our way,
Igniting hearts, come what may.

Celestial Trails in the Night's Embrace

Stars weave stories in the sky,
Whispers of ancient dreams arise.
Moonlit paths guide wandering souls,
Through the dark, their journey unfolds.

Galaxies dance in silent grace,
Time and space in a tender embrace.
Each twinkle holds a wish untold,
A universe of wonders unfolds.

The night reveals what daylight hides,
Mysteries where truth abides.
Constellations form a map for hearts,
In cosmic realms, the soul imparts.

Dreamers gaze with wonder's spark,
Finding light in the deepest dark.
With every breath, the night expands,
Connecting all through unseen hands.

So let your spirit take its flight,
On celestial trails of shimmering light.
In the night's embrace, we find our way,
Amidst the stars, forever we sway.

The Secret Language of Flickering Flames

In the hearth's warm, dancing glow,
Stories flicker, secrets flow.
Each flame a whisper of the past,
In its light, memories cast.

Crackling wood sings a lullaby,
Echoing dreams as embers fly.
A silent dialogue, old and wise,
Translating thoughts in the fire's eyes.

Shadows move with graceful ease,
As the fire's language seeks to please.
They twirl and sway, a rhythmic dance,
Inviting all to take a chance.

With every flicker, tales ignite,
Of love, of loss, of endless night.
The fire writes upon the air,
A timeless bond, a secret shared.

So gather close, take in the warmth,
Let the flames reveal their charm.
In this sacred space of light,
The soul finds peace in the quiet night.

A Stroll Through the Veils of Light

Step by step, where shadows play,
Veils of light guide the way.
A soft glow in the morning mist,
Nature beckons, can't resist.

In the glade, whispers of breeze,
Dance around the ancient trees.
Sunbeams scatter, paint the ground,
In this haven, joy is found.

Footfalls gentle on the earth,
Celebrate this sacred birth.
Each petal glistens, colors bright,
In the magic of pure light.

Meandering paths, a tranquil roam,
The world, a canvas, feels like home.
With each turn, new wonders greet,
In the light, my heart skips a beat.

So take a stroll and breathe it in,
Let this journey deep within.
Through veils of light, our spirits soar,
In every step, we find much more.

Crystals of Radiance in the Wilderness

In the wild, where silence reigns,
Crystals glimmer, break the chains.
Nature's jewels in sunlight's kiss,
A shimmering world, impossible to miss.

Through emerald leaves, they peek and gleam,
Reflecting dreams like a water's stream.
Dewdrops dance on blades of grass,
Each a treasure, too pure to pass.

Stones whisper stories of ancient lore,
Hold the secrets of times before.
With every hue and every shade,
In these crystals, wonders cascade.

Amidst the trees, a symphony plays,
As sunlight filters through the haze.
Nature's gallery, vibrant and vast,
A fleeting glimpse of shadows cast.

So wander through this sacred place,
Where crystals shine with gentle grace.
In the wilderness, let your heart rejoice,
For beauty speaks in nature's voice.

Radiance in the Midst of Shadows

In twilight's embrace, light softly sighs,
Flickering dreams beneath muted skies.
Whispers of hope in the dimly cast glow,
A dance of the brave where the dark waters flow.

Silhouettes linger, their edges defined,
Yearning for warmth in the chill of the blind.
Through veils of the night, a beacon appears,
Guiding lost souls with the strength of their fears.

A flicker ignites in the heart of the gray,
Illuminating paths that lead us away.
Turn shadows to light with a spark in your hand,
For every dark night has its own golden strand.

In moments of doubt, let your spirit abide,
Resilient and proud, with your truth as your guide.
The shadows may linger, but they cannot claim,
The light of your soul, forever aflame.

On Wings of Celestial Fire

A comet ignites in the vast cosmic sea,
Carving out dreams with wild ecstasy.
On wings of bright fire, we soar to the skies,
Where passions are born, where eternity lies.

Each flicker of stardust ignites our desire,
With hearts intertwined, we fuel the great fire.
Through galaxies spinning, we chase the unknown,
Together in flight, our spirits have grown.

To the rhythm of night, we find our true flight,
A tapestry woven of darkness and light.
In silence, we share our celestial embrace,
And lose ourselves deep in the timeless space.

Bound by the magic that fuels our ascent,
We journey on wings where the heavens are rent.
With eyes like the sun, and souls ever bright,
We dance 'neath the glow of the infinite light.

Unveiling the Hidden Glow

Beneath layers faded, a brilliance remains,
Woven in silence, like soft velvet chains.
In corners forgotten, there sparks a small fire,
Unveiling the glow of our innermost desire.

With patience we seek, through shadows we glance,
Finding the light in life's enigmatic dance.
Each moment revealing the treasures concealed,
As the heart opens wide, the truth is unsealed.

A flicker of kindness, a whisper of care,
Emerging from darkness, the light we all share.
In gardens of hope, let your spirit take root,
As the hidden glow blossoms, the soul bears sweet fruit.

So stand in the shadows, don't shy from the night,
For embedded in darkness, there's always a light.
As we unveil our glow, let the world feel the sweep,
Of the radiant journey that beckons from deep.

Portraits of Light Across Time

Canvas unframed, in colors divine,
Brush strokes of wisdom, where shadows entwine.
Each moment a portrait, each heartbeat a rhyme,
Telling stories of light across the vastness of time.

From dawn's gentle glow to the dusk's final breath,
We capture the essence of life and of death.
With memories painted, our legacies glow,
In the gallery of moments, we cherish and know.

The palette of ages reflects every hue,
In textures of laughter and tears we pursue.
Through corridors bright, the echoes resound,
As portraits of light find their home on the ground.

Let the past be our guide with its luminous spark,
Illuminating paths in the depth of the dark.
Together we'll weave all our stories in rhyme,
With portraits of light that transcend the confines of time.

Castles Illuminated by Starlight

In the hush of the night sky's embrace,
Castles rise with a majestic grace.
Their towers touch stars so bright,
Enchanted realms bathe in silver light.

Whispers of dreams linger in the air,
Soft echoes of laughter everywhere.
Moonlit paths guide the way,
Lost in wonder, we softly sway.

Golden banners flutter and dance,
In the glow, we find our chance.
To wander through tales time forgot,
In starlight's spell, we are caught.

Each stone tells a story of old,
Secrets and treasures that never grow cold.
Our hearts spark with dreams anew,
In castles where fairy tales come true.

As dawn's first light begins to rise,
The night fades with whispered sighs.
But the magic lingers deep inside,
In dreams of castles, we shall abide.

A Tidal Wave of Glimmering Moments

Waves crash with a glimmering sound,
Stories of life in treasures found.
Each splash a memory on the shore,
Whispers of joy, calling for more.

Under the moon's soft, tender light,
Every ripple dances, pure delight.
Time flows like sand through our hands,
Moments weave between life's strands.

We laugh, we cry, we soar with glee,
Caught in the tide, just you and me.
In every tide that comes and goes,
A glimmer of love forever glows.

The ocean sings a lullaby,
Under the stars, we dream and sigh.
With every wave, new journeys start,
A tidal wave, a beating heart.

As dawn breaks over the endless sea,
We chase the waves, wild and free.
Each moment a gem, brightly lit,
In our hearts, they forever fit.

Memories Enkindled by the Flame

In the flicker of firelight's glow,
Whispers of the past begin to flow.
Warmth wraps around us like a hug,
Memories dance in the softest snug.

Stories arise like embers bright,
Tales of love in the heart of night.
With each crackle, laughter unfolds,
And echoes of dreams that time holds.

The shadows play on the walls so tall,
Moments captured, we recall.
In the heart of the flame, we find,
A warmth that lingers in our mind.

With every spark, a wish takes flight,
A journey begun in the pale moonlight.
Together we sit, hand in hand,
In the glow of memories, we stand.

As the fire dies, and embers fade,
In our hearts, the memories are laid.
Though the flames may dim with time's embrace,
The warmth of the past holds a sacred place.

Bridging Worlds with Luminous Threads

In the tapestry of night, stars collide,
We weave our dreams with tides that guide.
Threads of light connect our hearts,
Bridging worlds where magic starts.

With each stitch, a story is spun,
Of laughter shared and battles won.
Luminous paths through shadows deep,
In each connection, our spirits leap.

Colors blend in the fabric of time,
Echoing rhythms, a beat in rhyme.
We dance along a celestial line,
Where dreams and reality intertwine.

Like constellations twinkling bright,
Each thread a whisper in the night.
In our hands, a universe grows,
Bridging worlds wherever love flows.

As dawn paints skies with golden hues,
These luminous threads will guide our views.
In every heart, a light will gleam,
Bridging worlds, fulfilling a dream.

The Horizon Where Dreams Ignite

At dawn's first blush, hopes take flight,
Brushstrokes of gold in morning light.
Whispers of futures softly call,
Chasing shadows, we rise, we fall.

The horizon glows, a canvas wide,
Where visions dance, and dreams reside.
With each step forward, hearts align,
In this boundless space, all stars combine.

Colors of courage paint the skies,
As fears dissolve, and faith complies.
We paint with passion, brush with care,
Framed in hope, we dare to dare.

A tapestry woven from wishes bright,
Threads of longing stitched in light.
In the distance, a flame ignites,
Guiding us safely through the nights.

Together we dream, hand in hand,
Building a castle in this land.
The horizon calls, with voices clear,
Hearts entwined, we conquer fear.

Celestial Currents in the Night Sky

Stars awaken, a silent choir,
Whispers of stardust, sparks of fire.
In the vastness, dreams take flight,
Guided by the moon's soft light.

Velvet skies hold secrets untold,
Mysteries waiting to unfold.
Comets trail with tales of old,
Of love and loss, of brave and bold.

Galaxies swirl in cosmic dance,
In every glance, a fleeting chance.
Nebulae bloom in colors spun,
Universes born, and time outrun.

Twinkling lights, a gentle sway,
Leading the lost in night's ballet.
Every pulse, a guiding star,
Drawing us close, no matter how far.

In this eternal, tranquil sea,
Our souls connect, wild and free.
Celestial currents drift and deep,
Carrying dreams on waves of sleep.

Fires of Transformation in Every Step

Embers flicker, igniting the path,
In the heart's furnace, we feel the wrath.
Ashes fall, but hope remains,
Building strength through joy and pains.

Each step forward, a blaze anew,
Sparks of courage, shining through.
We forge our way, hearts ablaze,
Through shadows and doubt, we learn to raise.

In the dance of change, we discover fire,
Passions ignite, taking us higher.
With every lesson, we rise to greet,
The fires of life with relentless beat.

So let the flames of growth unfold,
In the heat of challenges, hearts grow bold.
Transformation whispers, "Take a chance,"
And weave your fate in a vibrant dance.

From ashes we rise, resilient and bright,
Chasing the dawn, embracing the light.
Fires of transformation guide each step,
Leading us onward with every breath.

A Path of Flickering Memories

Down winding roads of yesteryears,
Whispers linger, echoing fears.
Footprints carved in time's embrace,
Memories flicker, filled with grace.

Each moment shines, a fleeting light,
Guiding us through the tender night.
Faces blurred, yet hearts stay clear,
In the tapestry we hold so dear.

Nostalgia threads through every lane,
Pictures alive, joy mixed with pain.
Lessons learned, love's gentle sway,
Illuminates our winding way.

As seasons change, the past unfolds,
Stories whispered, retold, and bold.
With each flicker, a truth we find,
A journey of heart, both kind and blind.

So walk the path, embrace the glow,
In flickering memories, wisdom flows.
Every heartbeat, a chapter spun,
In the book of life, we are one.

Beyond the Horizon's Glow

The stars begin to fade from sight,
As dawn unveils its gentle light.
A canvas bright, the sky aglow,
Awakens dreams from night's soft flow.

The whispers of the morning breeze,
Dance through the leaves of waking trees.
With every breath, a world begins,
Embracing hope, where love erupts.

Upon the path of golden rays,
Our hearts entwined, we find our ways.
Each step ignites a spark of fire,
To chase the dreams that never tire.

The ocean's tide meets sandy shore,
As waves collapse, they sing of more.
The horizon stretches far and wide,
With endless journeys, side by side.

In every color, life delights,
As we ignite the star-filled nights.
Beyond the horizon's endless glow,
Together through this life we'll flow.

Whispers of Light and Wonder

In shadows deep, where dreams reside,
A flicker glows, like hope inside.
It whispers softly, calls the heart,
To seek the truth, to make a start.

The moon above, a watchful guide,
Keeps secrets safe, where stars abide.
With every twinkle, thoughts await,
For light to illuminate our fate.

When darkness falls, and fears arise,
The whispers stir, they never lie.
Illuminated paths unfold,
With stories wrapped in dreams of gold.

In windy halls where echoes play,
We find the light in every sway.
To dance beneath the sky's embrace,
A journey shared, a sacred space.

With every breath, the magic spins,
Unraveling the world within.
In whispers calm, there's wonder near,
A tapestry of love and cheer.

The Luminescence of Our Steps

As twilight wraps the day in peace,
We venture forth, our hearts release.
Each step we take, a beam of light,
Illuminates the path of night.

In quiet corners, shadows play,
Our laughter echoes, come what may.
With every footfall, stories weave,
The tales we tell, what we believe.

Through fields adorned in silver sheen,
Our spirits soar, so wild and keen.
We chase the stars that dare to beam,
In the labyrinth of every dream.

The moonlight guides our journey true,
With every glance, I find in you.
The luminescence of our steps,
Creates a world that time redeems.

With hearts ablaze and hope in hand,
Together we will, forever stand.
In every stride, a promise flows,
Of love and light, where courage grows.

Odyssey of the Blazing Dawn

Awake, arise, the sun ascends,
A journey starts, the night-time bends.
With colors bright the day unfolds,
An odyssey of stories told.

The mountains echo songs of old,
With whispering winds, both shy and bold.
Each peak we climb, a new delight,
Our spirits dance in morning light.

As rivers flow and oceans roar,
We seek adventure, always more.
In unity, our hearts expand,
Together, we will make a stand.

The blazing dawn ignites our souls,
With every dream, our passion glows.
Through winding paths, where laughter rings,
We're woven strong, through everything.

In every heartbeat, life's embrace,
An odyssey in time and space.
Together, hand in hand we'll roam,
In blazing light, we've found our home.

Hues of the Infinite Beyond

In the twilight of dreams, colors collide,
A spectrum of thoughts where shadows reside.
Whispers of stars in cosmic embrace,
Each hue tells a tale in this boundless space.

Across the canvas of night, visions unfold,
Brushstrokes of passion, of stories untold.
Galaxies dance in a passionate flight,
As we drift in the hues of celestial light.

Through the silence, the universe sings,
A melody woven with vibrant strings.
Beyond the horizon, mysteries gleam,
In the whispers of color, we wander and dream.

Time stretches thin, as if to suspend,
Each moment alive, without need to pretend.
In the vastness, we seek and we find,
The hues of the infinite, enshrined in the mind.

So let us embrace this cosmic delight,
In the spectrum of dawn, we ignite the night.
With the palette of dreams, we hand in hand go,
To explore the infinite, with hearts all aglow.

Etched in Light on the Soul's Canvas

In the stillness, a whisper of grace,
Shimmers of light dance, framing our space.
Each flicker of hope, a mark on our soul,
A tapestry woven, making us whole.

Moments of laughter, etched in the dawn,
Eternal reminders, our fears gently gone.
With strokes of compassion, colors collide,
In the warmth of the heart, where shadows reside.

Every tear shed, a diamond's embrace,
Reflecting the journey, a sacred trace.
As time weaves its fabric, the threads intertwine,
In the glow of our memories, we brightly shine.

Through valleys of sorrow, peaks of delight,
Each step on this canvas, a dance in the light.
In the portrait of being, our spirits entwine,
Etched in the brilliance of love's perfect design.

So paint with your heart, let your colors run free,
In the masterpiece formed by just you and me.
On the canvas of life, every moment a chance,
To honor our stories, to joyfully dance.

Silent Roads of Shining Whispers

Beneath the stars, the roads gently weave,
Paths made of light, in which we believe.
Whispers of dreams echo softly at night,
Guiding our souls to a place of pure light.

In the quiet of moments, we wander alone,
Through the shimmering silence, our spirits have grown.
Each step on this journey, a tale yet to tell,
Along the still highways where secrets dwell.

Branches of hope stretch across the night sky,
Carrying wishes and wishes that fly.
In the hush of the twilight, we find the way,
Silent roads calling, urging us to stay.

Together, we travel, hearts open wide,
In the shimmer of whispers, there's nothing to hide.
Through valleys of patience, we gently glide,
On silent roads where our dreams can abide.

As dawn paints the horizon with brushes of gold,
We treasure the stories, the journeys retold.
On this vast road of endeavors and fears,
The shining whispers echo, calms all our tears.

Reflections of Light in the Eternal Now

In the mirror of time, reflections arise,
Moments of wonder, like stars in our eyes.
Fleeting yet timeless, they shimmer and glow,
In the fabric of now, where each breath flows.

Through the lens of the heart, we glimpse and we see,
The dance of existence, vibrant and free.
With every heartbeat, we cherish each spark,
In the shadow and light, we ignite the dark.

This harmony sings from the depths of the soul,
A melody whispered, making us whole.
As echoes of laughter blend with the sighs,
In the magic of now, all our hopes rise.

Through the pathways of thought, we wander and play,
In reflections of light, we find our way.
With each glowing moment, we gather, we grow,
In the landscape of being, we let our hearts flow.

Let us cherish the now, with its infinite grace,
In the radiance shared, we each find our place.
In reflections of light, we eternally vow,
To embrace this existence, the gift of the now.

Dance of the Radiant Wanderlust

In twilight's embrace, we twirl and glide,
Feet in harmony, hearts open wide.
Whispers of journeys on cool night air,
Stars beckon softly, guiding us there.

Cascading dreams in the moon's soft glow,
Every shadow echoes where we will go.
The compass of longing leads us anew,
Chasing horizons, just me and you.

With laughter as music, we map out the night,
Under luminous skies, everything feels right.
The pulse of the world dances with us too,
In this radiant rhythm, our spirits break through.

From mountains to valleys, the journey does call,
In every heartbeat, we answer it all.
Together we wander, together we soar,
In the dance of the wanderlust, forever explore.

Sunkissed Secrets of Infinite Roads

Beneath the clear sky, we chase the dawn,
Each road ahead, a promise drawn.
Sunkissed whispers carried on the breeze,
Unraveling secrets, setting hearts at ease.

With every mile, the horizon expands,
Stories of travelers linger in sands.
Through meadows and mountains, we carve our way,
Under the sun's glow, we'll seize the day.

Golden moments wrapped in laughter's embrace,
In the warmth of the light, we find our place.
Infinite roads stretch beyond our sight,
Guided by dreams, we venture into the light.

As dusk falls softly, the journey won't end,
For each step we take, new paths we can mend.
With hearts wide open and spirits unchained,
The sunkissed secrets of roads remain unchanged.

The Glow of Memories Yet to Be

In silent echoes of the past we tread,
Anticipating journeys, new stories ahead.
The glow of memories waits close at hand,
As we wander together, our dreams expand.

With every shared smile, a flicker ignites,
In the canvas of life, our colors take flight.
The heart's gentle whisper guides us with care,
Creating a tapestry, fragile yet rare.

The laughter we'll share, the moments we'll hold,
In this dance of life, both timid and bold.
Future embraces beckon, gently they plea,
For the glow of memories yet to be.

Through valleys of doubt and mountains of fear,
The beauty of knowing we always draw near.
With each heartbeat, we forge our own way,
In the glow of tomorrow, we'll cherish today.

Beneath the Canopy of Celestial Light

Underneath stars that shimmer and shine,
We find ourselves in a world divine.
The canopy stretches, a blanket of dreams,
Where wishes are woven in luminous seams.

As night whispers softly, secrets unfold,
Stories of starlight and love ever bold.
The universe dances, a spiraling waltz,
Beneath this vast sky, we dissolve our faults.

In the glow of the cosmos, we stand side by side,
Navigating the void with hearts open wide.
Each twinkle above tells of journeys in flight,
Awakening spirits beneath celestial light.

With every constellation, a promise is cast,
Binding our futures to shadows of past.
In this infinite space, together we soar,
Beneath the canopy of light, forever explore.

Beyond the Veil of Glistening Mists

A whisper glides through soft embrace,
Where dreams arise in hidden space.
Veils of mist, they dance and twirl,
In secret realms, our hopes unfurl.

Echoes shimmer, gently sway,
Guiding starlight through the gray.
Footsteps press on silken ground,
In quietude, our truth is found.

Shadows flit with moonlit grace,
Every heartbeat leaves a trace.
Venturing where few have gone,
Beyond the veil, we journey on.

Glistening streams of silver bright,
Illuminate the path of night.
In the mist, our spirits soar,
To the unknown, we seek and explore.

A tapestry of worlds unseen,
Woven threads in shades of green.
Here in wonder, we unite,
Beyond the veil, we seek the light.

Embracing the Glow of New Horizons

In dawn's embrace, the world awakes,
Golden rays on gentle lakes.
Fingers stretched towards the sun,
Every heartbeat, just begun.

Colors splash in vibrant views,
Nature's breath in tender hues.
Mountains rise, their shadows cast,
Embracing futures, free from past.

Winds of change, a soothing balm,
Carrying dreams, soft and calm.
With each step, we leave behind,
All that binds, a new world to find.

Horizons beckon, drawing near,
Every whisper loud and clear.
As we journey, hearts ignite,
Embracing the glow, our spirits bright.

Together we will rise and soar,
Chasing dreams forevermore.
In the light, our stories blend,
Onward to horizons without end.

Luminescence in the Heart of the Abyss

In darkness deep, where shadows creep,
A flicker glows, secrets to keep.
Stars ignite in endless night,
Guiding souls to find the light.

Whispers linger, soft and low,
Echoes of what we yearn to know.
In the depths, courage blooms,
From despair, new hope resumes.

Abyssal depths, a silent song,
Within the dark, we all belong.
As shadows dance, hearts intertwine,
In the void, our spirits shine.

Fathom deep, there lies a spark,
Illuminating paths so stark.
With every breath, we brave the night,
In the void, we find our light.

Together we rise, defying fate,
In the abyss, we find our fate.
For in darkness, hope persists,
Luminescence in the heart of mists.

Chronicles of the Opalescent Path

Written in the stars above,
Tales of wonder, tales of love.
Opalescent dreams descend,
Along the path where journeys blend.

Footprints left in grains of time,
Every step a silent rhyme.
Winding roads through light and shade,
Chronicles of choices made.

With every dawn, a story grows,
In whispered winds, our spirit flows.
Guided by the moon's soft glow,
On opalescent paths we go.

Nature sings a timeless song,
Every note where we belong.
Through valleys low and mountains high,
The chronicles of life pass by.

Hand in hand, we'll write our fate,
In each moment, love dictates.
As the stars begin to twine,
Opalescent paths align.

Pathway of Luminous Echoes

Footsteps tread on silken light,
Whispers dance in softest night,
Each shadow glows, a fleeting spark,
Guiding hearts through twilight's dark.

Winding paths of dreams untold,
Where secrets sigh and secrets unfold,
The air is thick with magic's breath,
Binding life with threads of death.

Stars above in silent gaze,
Mark the journey through the haze,
Reality and dream align,
In the glow of worlds divine.

Echoes of the past remain,
Fading softly like soft rain,
Each memory, a boundless sea,
Flowing gently, wild and free.

Hold the light upon your face,
As you walk through time and space,
With every step, a whispered call,
To the echoes, one and all.

Glimmers Along the Infinite Trail

A winding road through spark and shroud,
Glimmers shine, both bright and loud,
Each step a beacon in the night,
Filling souls with pure delight.

Whispers carried on the streams,
Floating softly, like fragile dreams,
The air is laced with shimmering sound,
In every corner, magic's found.

Footprints left in glowing dust,
Trust the path, embrace the trust,
With each heartbeat, spirits rise,
Underneath the velvet skies.

Chasing shadows, weaving light,
Life's a dance, from dark to bright,
Echoes linger, softly sway,
Guiding travelers on their way.

In that glow, the hearts align,
Through the maze, your spirit shines,
Every glimmer, a sacred sign,
On this path, your soul is mine.

Dance of the Shimmering Souls

Underneath the moon's embrace,
Souls entwined in timeless grace,
With each turn, a joyous leap,
Awakening the dreams we keep.

In the light of stars, we spin,
Every note, a dance within,
Whispers of the night ignite,
Spirits soaring, taking flight.

Through the shadows, colors blend,
In this realm, we all transcend,
Harmony in every sigh,
In the echoes, we comply.

With each beat, our hearts collide,
In the rhythm, we confide,
Shimmering under cosmic skies,
In this dance, our essence flies.

Embrace the glow, let worries fade,
In the light, our love displayed,
Every moment, a timeless song,
Where the shimmering souls belong.

Celestial Wayfarers

We wander through the cosmic sea,
As celestial wayfarers, wild and free,
Chasing dreams that twirl and glide,
In the stardust, we confide.

Galaxies whisper secrets old,
As we traverse through tales untold,
Each journey woven, sacred thread,
With every step, our hearts are fed.

Constellations spark a flame,
Guiding us, we are the same,
Through the void, our spirits dance,
In the light, we take a chance.

Hands entwined with fate's design,
In this realm, our souls align,
Every star a story bright,
Illuminating our shared flight.

Close your eyes, feel the embrace,
Of the universe's gentle grace,
As wayfarers in the night,
Together, we become the light.

Horizon's End

The sun dips low, a fiery glow,
Whispers of night begin to flow.
Shadows stretch, the day retreats,
In this moment, time discreet.

Horizon's End

Colors blend in twilight's embrace,
Stars ignite, they take their place.
The world fades soft, a gentle sigh,
As dreams and darkness intertwine.

Horizon's End

Footsteps trail on empty sands,
The sea calls out with open hands.
In solitude, the heart will mend,
At the edge of light, where day may end.

Horizon's End

A final beam, a whispered cheer,
Promises made, now disappear.
With every breath, a new refrain,
In twilight's arms, all loss is gain.

Horizon's End

The sky a canvas, painted vast,
Echoes of moments fading fast.
In the silence, peace will blend,
With hopes renewed, at horizon's end.

Dawn's Beginning

A soft light breaks, the dark unwinds,
Morning stirs, the night unwinds.
Birds sing sweet in trees so green,
A world reborn, fresh and serene.

Dawn's Beginning

Golden rays kiss the waking earth,
Whispers of hope, a new rebirth.
Dreams take flight on zephyr's wings,
Embracing all the joy life brings.

Dawn's Beginning

The dew glistens on blades of grass,
Time slows down as moments pass.
With every heartbeat, light cascades,
In dawn's embrace, the shadows fade.

Dawn's Beginning

A canvas painted with morning hues,
A promise kept in vibrant views.
Nature's chorus, a sweet refrain,
In dawning light, there's naught but gain.

Dawn's Beginning

In gentle whispers, the day awakes,
With every breath, the spirit breaks.
In this dawn, pure magic sings,
A world renewed where hope takes wing.

A Voyage Among the Illuminated

Into the night, a journey calls,
Guided by stars, their shimmering thralls.
The moonlight dances on waves so blue,
In silence deep, dreams come true.

A Voyage Among the Illuminated

A ship of thoughts sails through the dark,
Every heartbeat, a glowing spark.
Every tide will tell its tale,
Of distant lands and winds so frail.

A Voyage Among the Illuminated

Reflections twinkle on sapphire seas,
Whispers carried by gentle breeze.
Each star a story, a fate entwined,
In this voyage, worlds aligned.

A Voyage Among the Illuminated

With open hearts, we chart the night,
Navigating by the soft moonlight.
Every glimmer a guiding thread,
In the tapestry of dreams, we're led.

A Voyage Among the Illuminated

As dawn approaches, shadows wane,
A journey's end, yet not in vain.
For every star, a truth we seek,
In our voyage, horizons speak.

The Sundrenched Labyrinth

Paths entwined in golden light,
A maze of joy, both wild and bright.
Every turn, a tale unfolds,
In secrets whispered, life beholds.

The Sundrenched Labyrinth

Amidst the blooms, a fragrant air,
Lost in wonder, without a care.
Sunbeams filter through the leaves,
In this haven, the spirit weaves.

The Sundrenched Labyrinth

A dance of colors, vibrant hues,
Every step brings forth new views.
In laughter shared, time seems to freeze,
In the labyrinth, hearts find ease.

The Sundrenched Labyrinth

Echoes linger of joy and peace,
In nature's arms, worries cease.
With every twist, a chance to grow,
In this sunlit path, love will flow.

The Sundrenched Labyrinth

As shadows stretch and evening nears,
Memories linger, laughter cheers.
In this maze of light we blend,
With open hearts, a world to mend.

Wandering Through Brazen Beams

In bustling streets where sunlight streams,
We wander wide, chasing dreams.
The city's pulse, a vibrant tune,
Under the warmth of afternoon.

Wandering Through Brazen Beams

Sidewalks shine in golden rays,
Each moment a dance, a fleeting gaze.
In laughter shared, we come alive,
In this bright world, we thrive.

Wandering Through Brazen Beams

With every step, the stories grow,
In busy lanes and rivers slow.
Footprints marked on paths unknown,
In brazen beams, our spirits shone.

Wandering Through Brazen Beams

As twilight fades, the stars awake,
In every heart, a dream we make.
Through vibrant streets, we roam and play,
In golden sun, we're led astray.

Wandering Through Brazen Beams

In the city's arms, under vast sky,
We search for meaning, wondering why.
Yet every hour, a gift unspun,
In brazen beams, our lives are one.

Reflections in the Prism of Time

In the glass of memories so clear,
Moments flicker, whispering near.
Shadows dance on the walls of the past,
Echoes of laughter, forever to last.

Faces fade in the soft, golden light,
Each one a story, a tale of delight.
Through the lens of the heart, we see,
Time's gentle touch, a sweet reverie.

Fragments of joy, woven like lace,
In the tapestry of time, we find our place.
While seasons shift, like the winds that blow,
In the prism of now, our true colors glow.

Moments suspended in delicate space,
Reflections of love that time can't erase.
In the silence between breaths we make,
Life's precious journey, the paths we take.

As clocks turn softly, we learn to embrace,
Each fleeting second, a sacred grace.
With every heartbeat, we shimmer and shine,
Chasing the light in the prism of time.

Glimmers in the Fabric of Existence

Threads of starlight weave through the night,
In the fabric of life, they shimmer bright.
Every soul a stitch, each heart a tune,
Together we rise, like flowers in bloom.

In dreams unfurling, visions appear,
Glimmers of hope that dissolve every fear.
With whispers of kindness, the world we mend,
Linking our stories, each bend with a friend.

Colors collide in vibrant embrace,
Painting our journeys, each line, every trace.
In the dance of the cosmos, we find our way,
Glimmers of light in the night and the day.

Moments of laughter, times of despair,
We gather the fragments, we learn to repair.
In the heart of existence, love's gentle call,
Glimmers together, we rise, never fall.

In the weave of the universe, threads intertwine,
Creating a tapestry that's yours and mine.
In every soft whisper, in every loud cheer,
Glimmers of existence will always be near.

Trails of the Incandescent Wanderer

Footprints in stardust, a path yet unknown,
The wanderer journeys where wild winds have blown.
With lanterns of dreams, they light up the dark,
Following starlight, igniting a spark.

In valleys of echoes, through mountains of blue,
They weave through the shadows, embracing what's true.
With a heart like a compass, forever they roam,
Finding the magic, wherever they call home.

Through rivers of time, they sail with the breeze,
Collecting the whispers of trees in the seas.
With every horizon, new stories unfold,
Trails of the wanderer, adventurous and bold.

In silence and thunder, they dance on the edge,
With courage like fire, they never allege.
Their smile, a beacon, igniting the night,
The incandescent wanderer, glowing with light.

So let the winds guide them, let the stars sing,
In the trails of their journey, the joy they bring.
With hearts full of wonder, they'll travel afar,
The incandescent wanderer, a luminous star.

The Spectrum of Hidden Realms

Beyond what we see, the colors collide,
In hidden dimensions where secrets abide.
Each hue tells a story, a silent refrain,
In the spectrum's embrace, there's joy and there's pain.

Through shadows and light, dimensions expand,
Whispers of magic flow through every hand.
In the silence of worlds, where dreams intertwine,
The spectrum of realms, each one a design.

With every heartbeat, a portal appears,
Leading us gently through laughter and tears.
In the tapestry woven from all that we find,
The spectrum of life binds us, intertwined.

As colors awaken the depths of our soul,
We journey through realms that make us feel whole.
In the dance of existence, we learn to embrace,
The spectrum of moments, a shared, sacred space.

Through layers of reality, we take our flight,
Exploring the wonders that shimmer in sight.
In the depth of our hearts, we'll always prevail,
In the spectrum of hidden, colorful trails.

Glowing Footprints on the Fabric of Time

In twilight's haze where dreams ignite,
Footprints shimmer, soft and bright.
Echoes whisper through the night,
Marking paths of faded light.

Moments linger, soft and rare,
Each a treasure, beyond compare.
Stories woven with tender care,
In every step, memories share.

Patterns dance in cosmic tune,
Each one fades, a silent rune.
Time moves on, a fleeting boon,
While glowing trails merge with the moon.

Every heartbeat, every sigh,
Paints the canvas of the sky.
Glowing footprints never die,
In the chambers where dreams lie.

Threads of gold and shades of grey,
Composed in night's intricate play.
Past and future intertwine their say,
Glowing footprints, they won't stray.

The Eternal Dance of Light and Shadow

In the twilight's gentle sway,
Light and shadow come to play.
Flickering forms in bright display,
Whispers of night, and then the day.

A waltz performed on moonlit grounds,
Graceful patterns, softening sounds.
Echoed laughter, joy abounds,
In the silence, magic founds.

Illuminated dreams in flight,
Chasing echoes of pure light.
Shadows dance, a fleeting sight,
Embracing darkness, out of sight.

The harmony of dusk and dawn,
Crafts a tapestry well drawn.
In every breath, a connection spawned,
The eternal dance, life's sweet yawn.

Through cycles vast, where spirits gleam,
Light and shadow share their dream.
A symphony of life's esteem,
In every heart, love's gentle beam.

Revelations Beneath the Silver Glow

Beneath the moon, secrets unfold,
Silent stories, whispers bold.
In silver light, the truth bestowed,
Revelations softly told.

Mysteries lie in night's embrace,
Stars entwined in cosmic lace.
Each reflection, a sacred space,
Glimmers of hope, a tender trace.

Time stands still, as dreams unwind,
In the night, what will you find?
Heartbeats echo, intertwined,
In the depths of the mind.

Moonlit paths invite the brave,
To seek the solace that will save.
Underneath the silver wave,
Every soul, a light to crave.

In twilight's arms, the silence flows,
With every star, a story glows.
Revelations through the shadows,
Embrace the night, let wonder grow.

Rapture of the Cosmic Sojourn

In the silence of the night,
Stars ignite, a wondrous sight.
They beckon forth with soft delight,
Rapture born from cosmic flight.

Galaxies swirl in grand embrace,
Infinite wonders, endless space.
Every heartbeat, a cosmic trace,
Journeying through time and place.

Waves of stardust paint the skies,
A celestial dance that never dies.
Truths unveiled in moonlit lies,
As galaxies whisper and rise.

Every traveler finds their way,
In rapture of the night and day.
Through the cosmos, dreams convey,
A sojourn that will never fray.

In the vastness, we take our part,
Navigating with open heart.
The cosmic rapture, a work of art,
A journey shared from the start.

www.ingramcontent.com/pod-product-compliance
Ingram Content Group UK Ltd.
Pitfield, Milton Keynes, MK11 3LW, UK
UKHW021424220125
4239UKWH00039B/514

9 781805 617976